DISORDER IN THE AMERICAN COURTS

REAL QUOTES FROM ACTUAL COURT PROCEEDINGS
2014 EDITION

EDITED AND COMPILED
BY MARCELLE BOREN
ILLUSTRATIONS BY E.H. SHEPARD

Illustrations are from the original work, *The Wind in the Willows*, published in 1908, and now reside in the public domain. Many thanks to E.H. Shepard for the beauty his art brought to our world.

Published by Iwahu Publishing
For information on ordering, please email us at
iwahupublishing@gmail.com

ISBN-13: 978-0692274576
ISBN-10: 069227457X

The following quotes are things people actually said under oath in legal court proceedings. Some proper names and place names have been changed to protect the guilty until proven innocent.

CONTENTS

PART 1: MEMORY

Well, I can't say right now I just remember it off the top of my remembrance.

I tend to really wash these things out of my head after they're over because there's not room for all that stuff to stick around.

Tell me the ones
you don't recall.

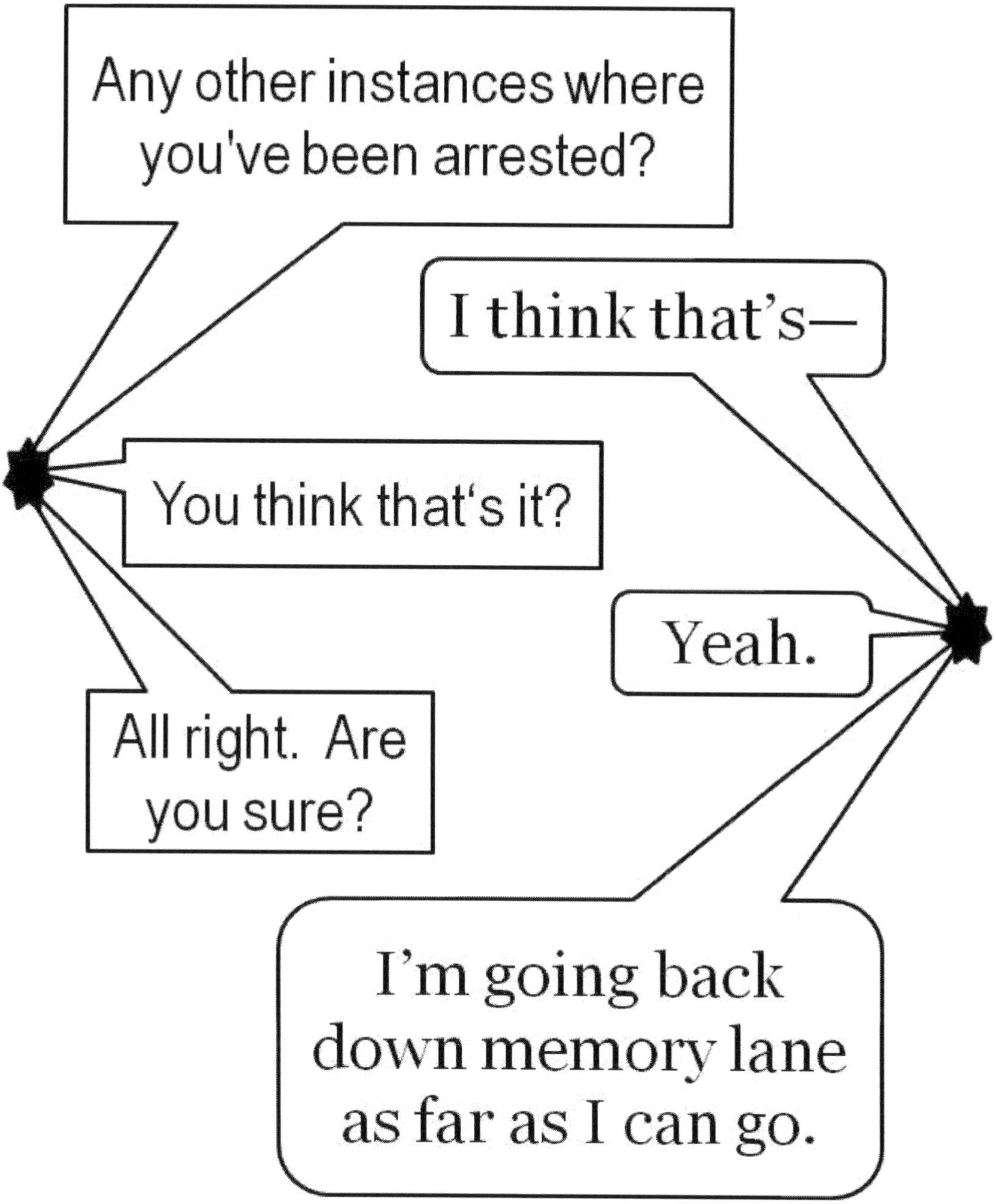
Any other instances where you've been arrested?
I think that's—
You think that's it?
Yeah.
All right. Are you sure?
I'm going back down memory lane as far as I can go.

And I don't remember if the chicken came before the egg or not.

I work all – I really – takes me all day to clean my house, but I think it's because I forget what I'm doing, you know.

I'm just asking what you can remember.

My butt wasn't showing. I recall that.

I'm just asking for your best recollection, sir.

I wouldn't call it my best memory. But it's my spur-of-the-moment memory right now.

Tell me everything you can recall about that conversation.

Well, I can tell you it was nighttime. I don't know what time of day.

And who is the author or authors of that?

Oh, there's many. And I wish I could remember all of them. I can't, but I'm one of them. That's the only one I remember.

PART 2: PLANES, TRAINS & AUTOMOBILES

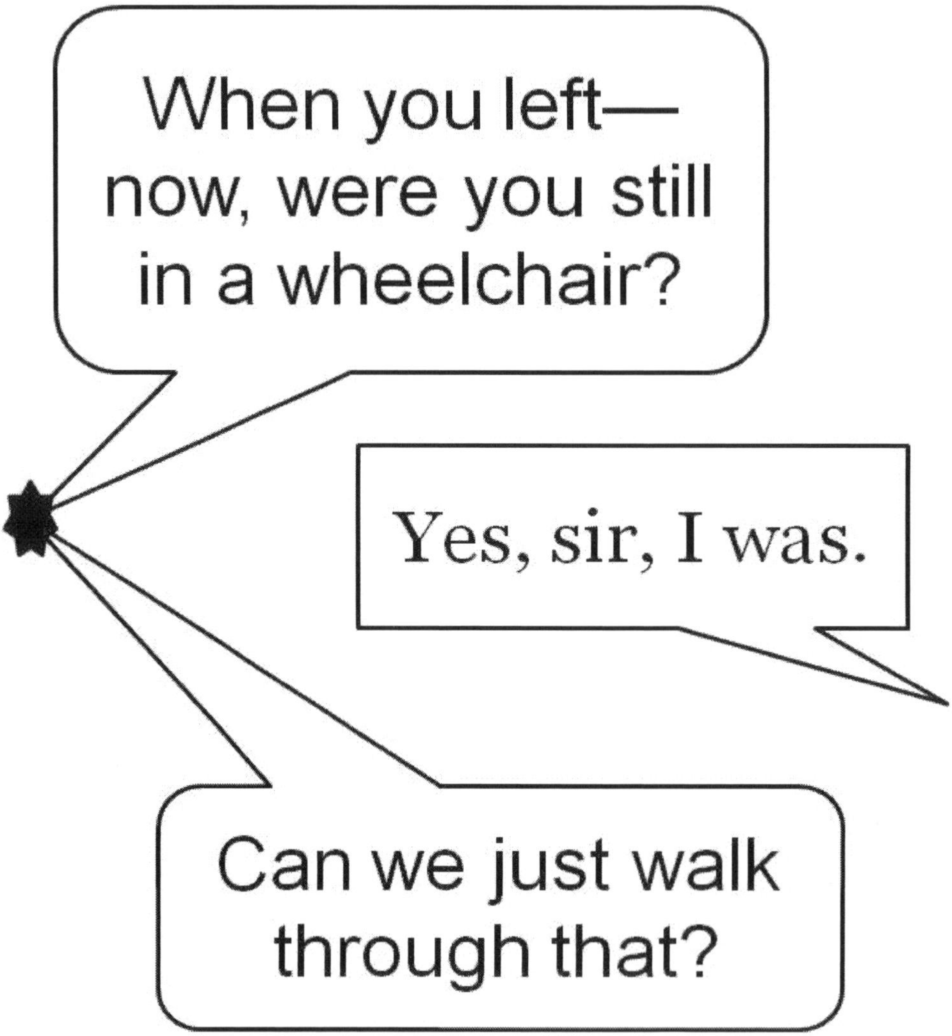
When you left—
now, were you still
in a wheelchair?
Yes, sir, I was.
Can we just walk
through that?

Why did you purchase a new truck in 2004?

Well, I was having problematic problems.

Have your injuries and what you've gone through been hard on your family, your wife and the girls?

Very hard.

How so? Tell me about that.

I sold my Harley.

Well, tell me about that road. Was it bumpy? Was it curvy? Was it—were there hills?

We're talking about Oklahoma roads.

And you only get one life, but you get tons of cars.

If our pilot were blind, it wouldn't make a difference to you from the standpoint of your visibility study. Is that true?

I would have an opinion about what a blind pilot could see. Yes, I would.

PART 3: ANATOMY AND PHYSIOLOGY

Prior to this accident, had you had a situation where you had any type of injury where you had to go see a doctor for an injury?

Well, it was, like, about 10 or 12 years ago, I went through a stomach virus; and he gave me some Mylanta. And that took care of that. He said it was gas.

And then I kind of went, "Ah, that's probably the reason for my odor."

She complained that for a while there her kidneys started working again. She could urinate on her own. And that was a plus, we thought.

My mother kept up
with all of her supplies
that she needed for her
urostomy and her
colostomy bag. And
she was very anal
about getting her stuff.

What problems do you still have with the right shoulder?

I have a lot of problems trying to raise it up over my waist.

There's a yes hand and a right hand; okay?

When you twisted your ankle, where did you have the sensation of any pain?

In the ankle.

When you said "knees," as in both knees?

On a worst-case scenario, what—how would you rate the pain in your lower back?

Say an eight.

And how often does that occur?

When it decides to do it.

Any other parts of your body that were injured?

That's the only—just all over.

My head was very big.

PART 4:
ACCIDENTS

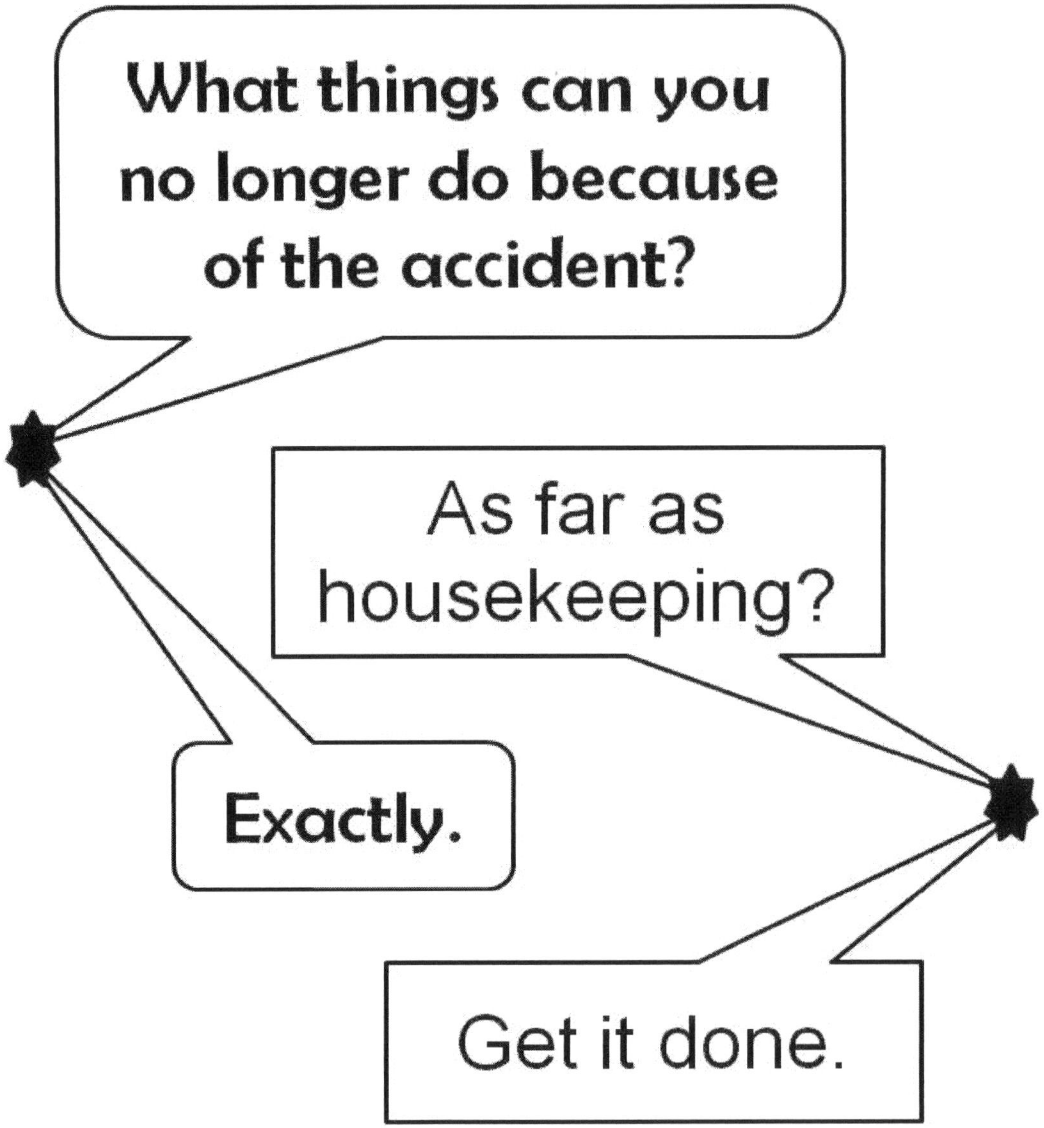
What things can you no longer do because of the accident?
As far as housekeeping?
Exactly.
Get it done.

How many times did your car spin around?

I don't know. I just hung on. Maybe—I think I was facing the other direction a little more than usual.

Did Ms. Short say anything before the accident happened about, "There's going to be an accident," or, "Look out," or any—yell or anything?

She said, yeah, "We're fixing to" –you know, as we—you know, as we're fixing to hit her, she said, "We're fixing to hit her."

Any other body parts at the scene of the accident that we need to talk about?

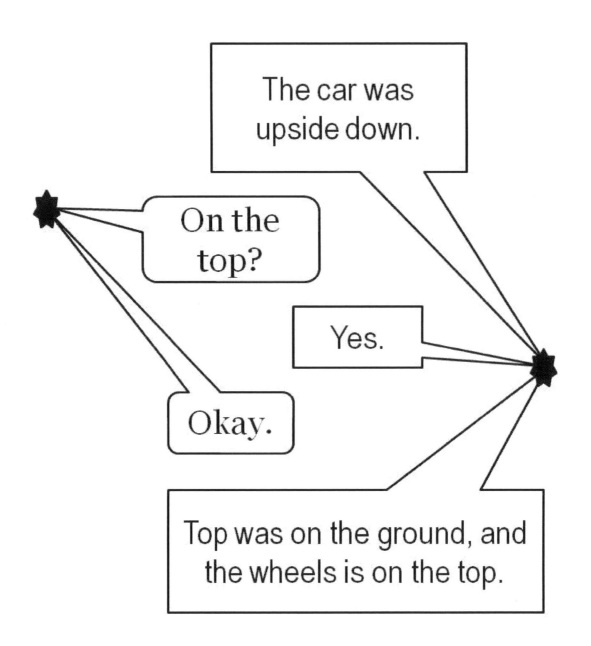

PART 5: ALL IN A
DAY'S WORK

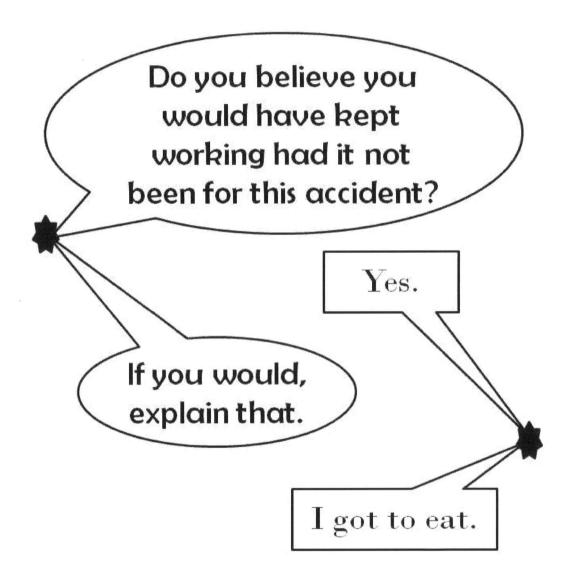

We do that with -- you know, that's normal practice, when somebody gets caught in damn stupidity, you march them out of the door. You don't sit and negotiate.

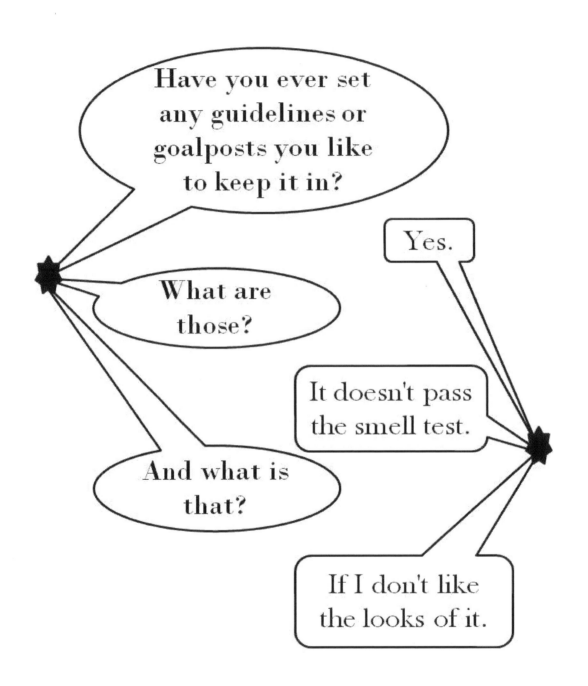

And over the past 30 years, have you been doing surgery that entire time, sir?

Yes.

Would you say it's
a better design,
the new design?

Well, I personally
think it's a better
design because
it's—I did it.

Sue had a job at the hatchery to do. Her job was to stay on top of everything in that hatchery.

And what was your job title?

Upholstery.

I shut it down, like, two and a half years ago. Eternal Supply, I shut it down.

You observed administrators observing you; is that right?

Do you have any person you turn your logs in to specifically?

We put them in an envelope and put the envelope in the basket. And then they go -- somebody in the office goes through. I don't know who.

It's the log fairy.

Do you have a back office at that store?

No. Got a bathroom.

PART 6:
Q & A

It's my job to ask questions. It's your job to understand them.

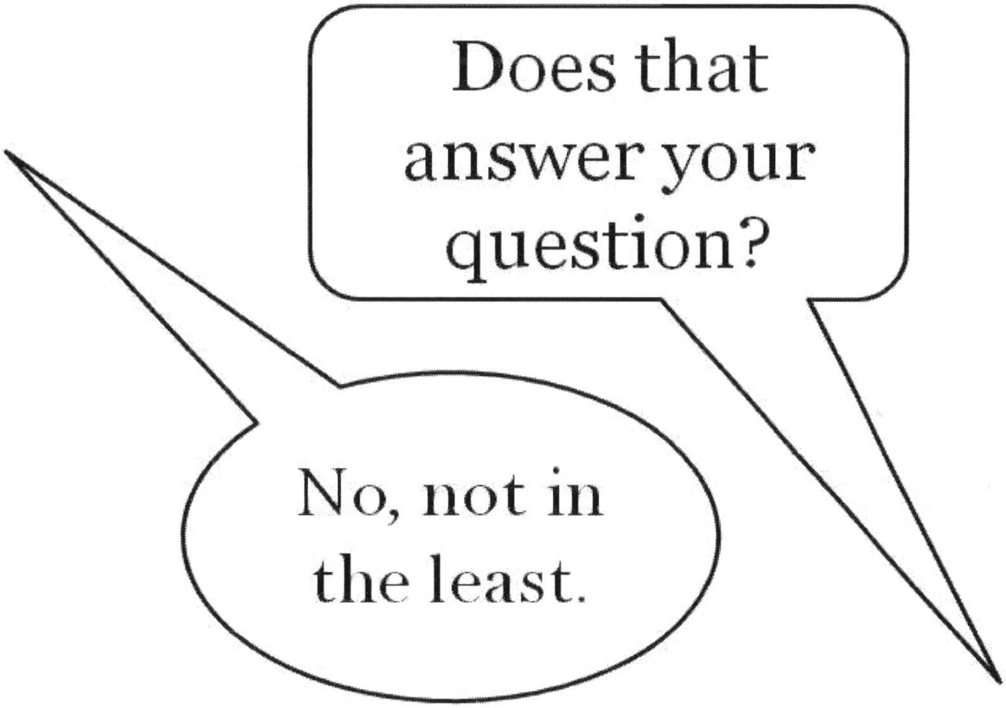
Does that answer your question?
No, not in the least.

Well, let's start with the questions first before we get to the response.

I need to make sure
that I don't answer
correctly, because there
are a number of
categories on here.

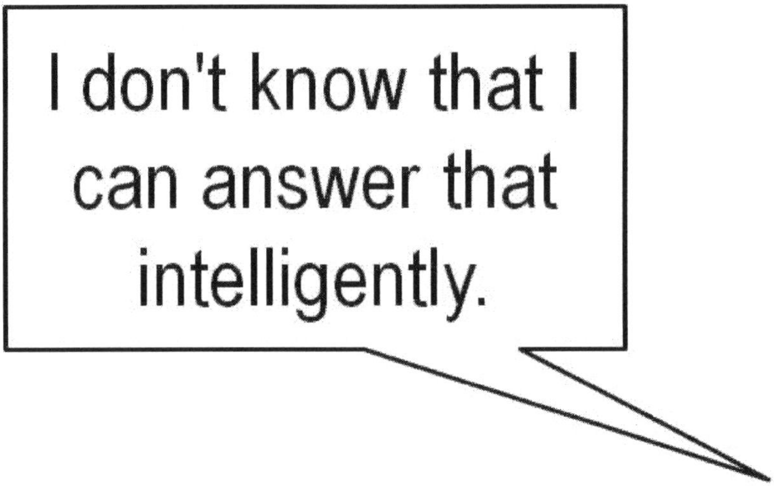
I don't know that I can answer that intelligently.

Doctor, I appreciate your answer, but it didn't even touch my question.

I looked over several spreadsheets we provided, and I believe these were the ones that meet the constraints of your question.

I think that's engineer talk for, "I've answered your question."

Some of my questioning and your answering are not quite tracking.

Let me ask
another series of
stupid questions.

I'm sorry. You've lost me in the question. I'm sorry.

Okay. Well, I almost lost myself. So, fair comment.

So I'm going to ask you questions, and hopefully they will be intelligible. Hopefully, each question will be slightly different, as well. That doesn't always happen, but I have an expectation that that will occur.

I'm going to have to limit my questions because my bridge just came off of my tooth.

You can
say yes?

Yes.

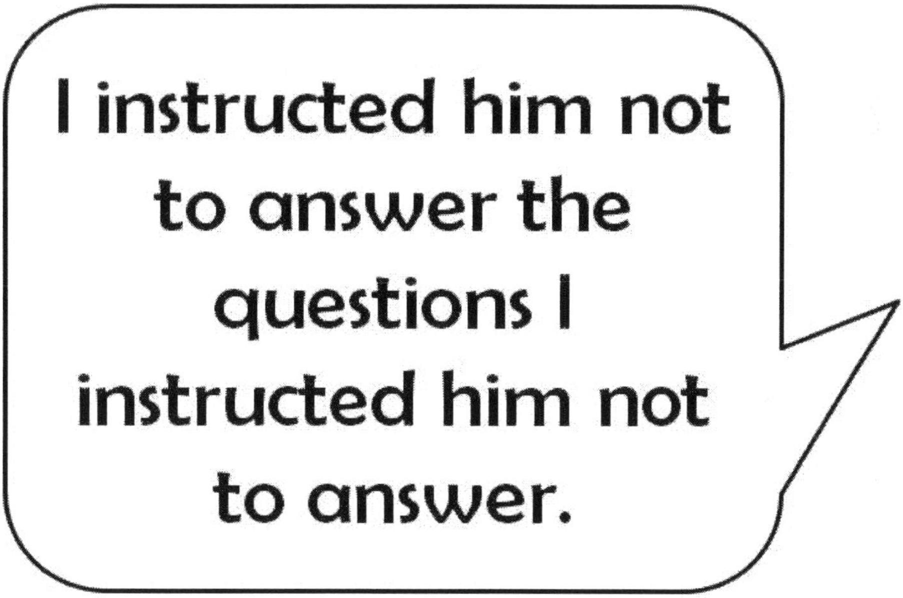
I instructed him not to answer the questions I instructed him not to answer.

PART 7:
ANIMALS

Alexandra's the elephant in the room right now. You know that, right?

What do you keep above the machine on those shelves?

Wine glasses and some other pet items.

We have a Buffalo herd, too. They would be running through fences and people's yards, and that's not good for public relations.

How far away
was the Rhino
when you
inherited it?

Do you still own the three horses?

Yes, sir. You want to buy one?

PART 8:
MONEY MATTERS

I just put down "59 inches," like, 12 times 5.

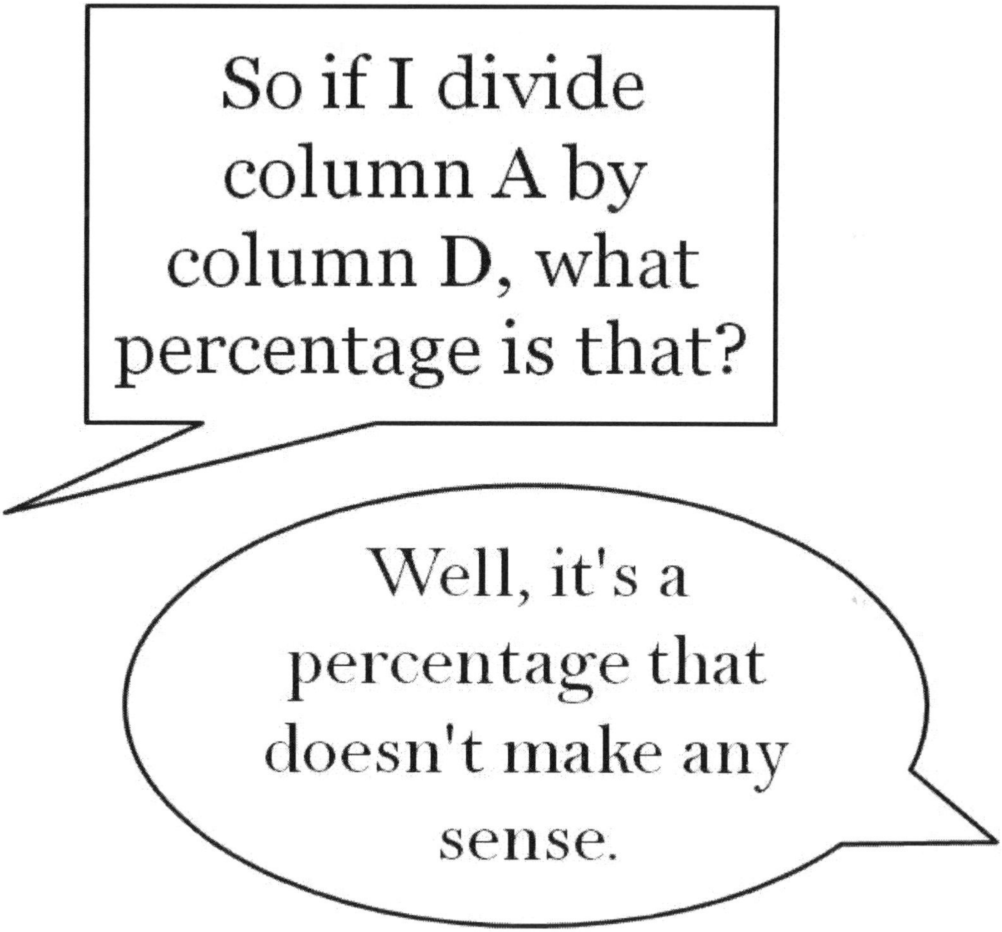
So if I divide column A by column D, what percentage is that?
Well, it's a percentage that doesn't make any sense.

I don't put no property value on junk.

Not to be flip, but how often do you get a letter that says you may have potential liability in $1.7 million?

Hopefully not very often.

Two plus two did equal four this time. Sometimes doesn't.

You guys are handling customer credit card accounts and you're handling floral shop bank accounts and stuff like that, so you have security programs in place to prevent hacking; right?

Yes. Well, the bank accounts not so much.

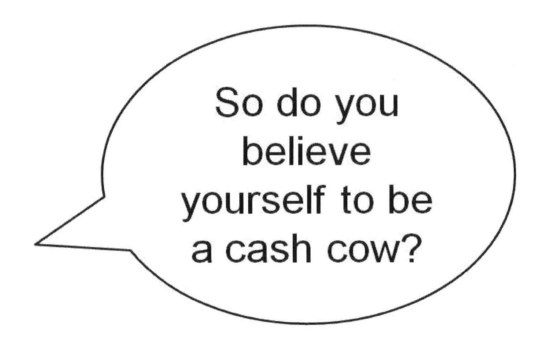

Do you know what your credit score is now?

Probably below the ocean.

What does a finance advisor do?

Well, he the one would find where would we, you know, get the loans from, the—you know, "Where's the money at?" And to—you know, to build the company the right way. He the one.

Well, a bank wouldn't be liable for money stolen from it. The thief would be liable to return the money to the bank.

PART 9: PLANNING AND PAPERWORK

Can you describe for me what those documents are?

They're painful.

You want to mess somebody up, just mark something one, two and four and spend the rest of the day looking for three.

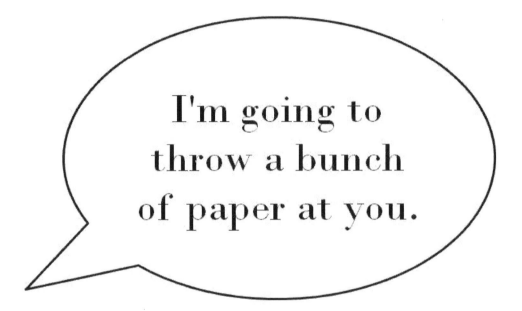

Well, there's a yes and a no box now. And do you choose the "yes" box, the "no" box, or "I don't know" box?

I choose the "it depends on the circumstances" box.

Did you prepare this schedule yourself?

Under my direction, yes.

PART 10:
MARRIAGE

I need to get out of the house. For my wife's sake partly.

So you ended that relationship at that time. Is that what you're saying?

No, no. We stayed together and divorced.

And did you learn that he was gay after you married him?

No.

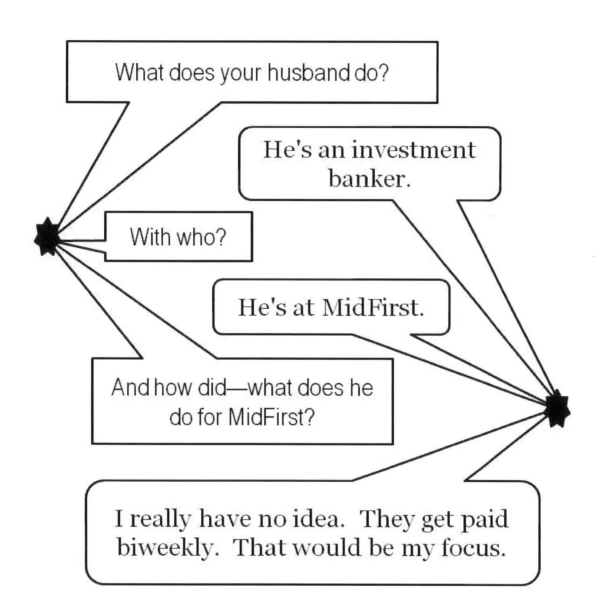

And who—what was the name of your—ex-husband, I'm assuming?

Same as my husband now.

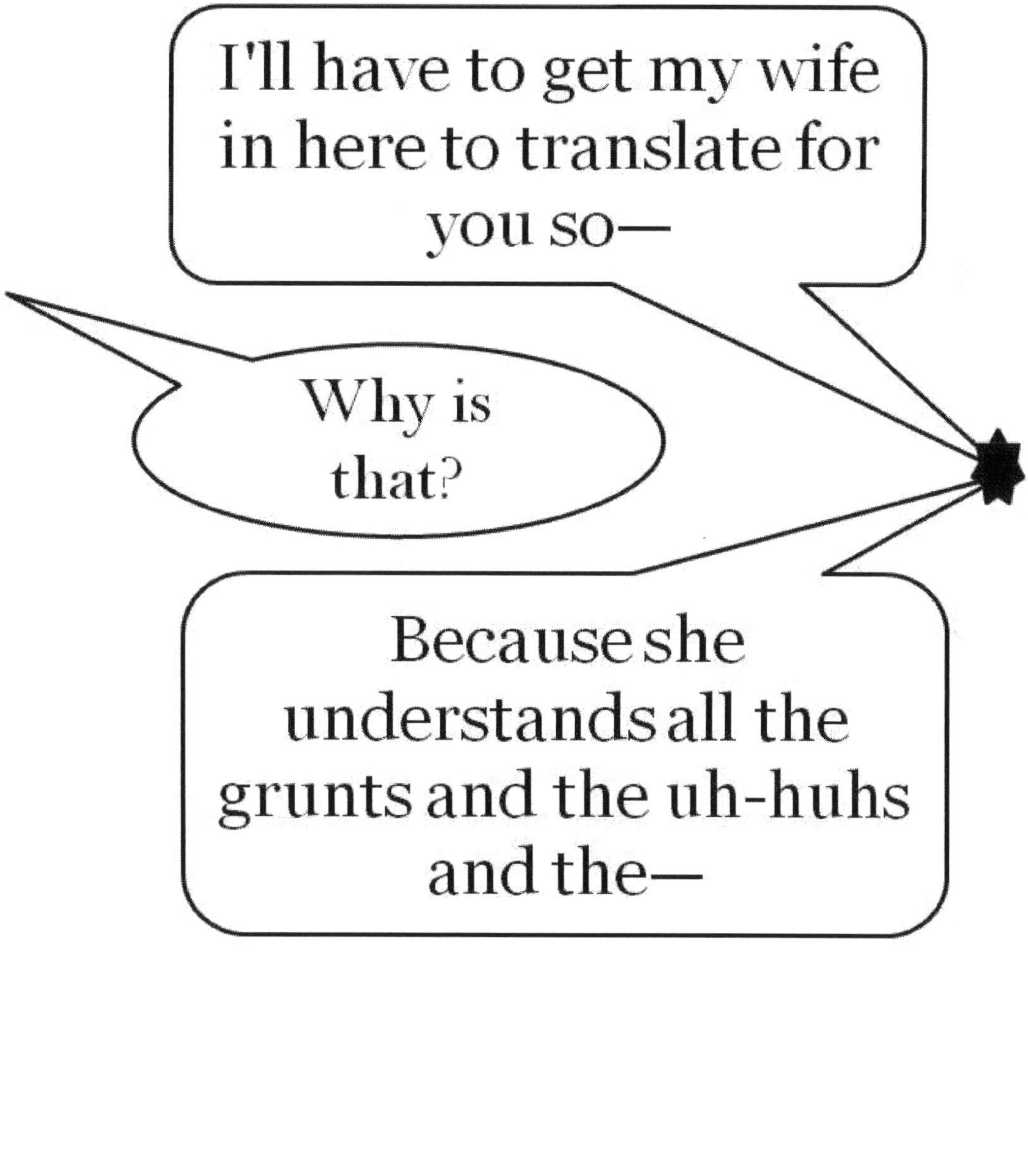
I'll have to get my wife in here to translate for you so—
Why is that?
Because she understands all the grunts and the uh-huhs and the—

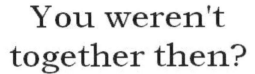

You weren't together then?

Not together. We were together, but I wasn't with her.

All right. Thanks for clearing that up for me.

Ma'am, are you married currently?
Yeah. Kind of. No. Not really. Sort of.

And your husband said that he didn't have anything to do with this, that he did what you told him to do.

And I appreciate him for that.

Were you aware of any of the details of any prior marriage that Peter had?

I know he was married once, but I have no idea even what her name was. I don't even know what she looked like. But I was at the wedding.

PART 11:
KNOWLEDGE IS POWER

I know what
I know from
what I know.

Do you know the month of any year?

Do you have any other businesses other than those two?

Not to my knowledge, no.

So there's a difference between what you know here and now and what you know some other time?

I know nothing about this, so I'm sure to say something stupid.

Did he give you information?

He gave us partial information.

Okay. What did he not give you?

Just about anything meaningful.

I don't know exactly—the exact—I don't know exactly the figures and exactly what we paid out. I don't know exactlies, sir. I just don't know.

No. Not that I recall. You keep asking that one. Do you know something I don't know?

PART 12:
STATING THE OBVIOUS

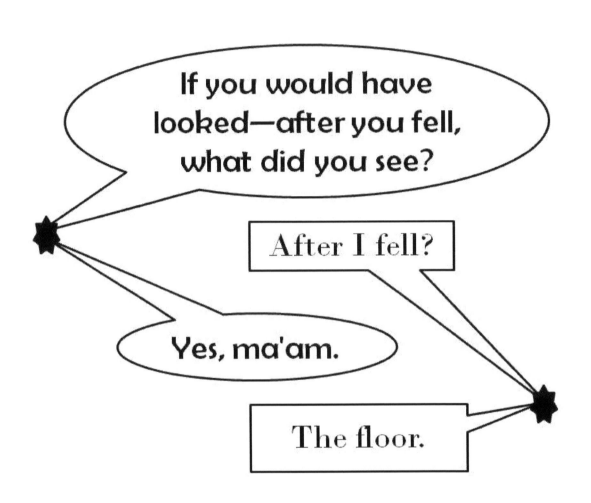

That part of the form would be completed by the individual that is completing the form.

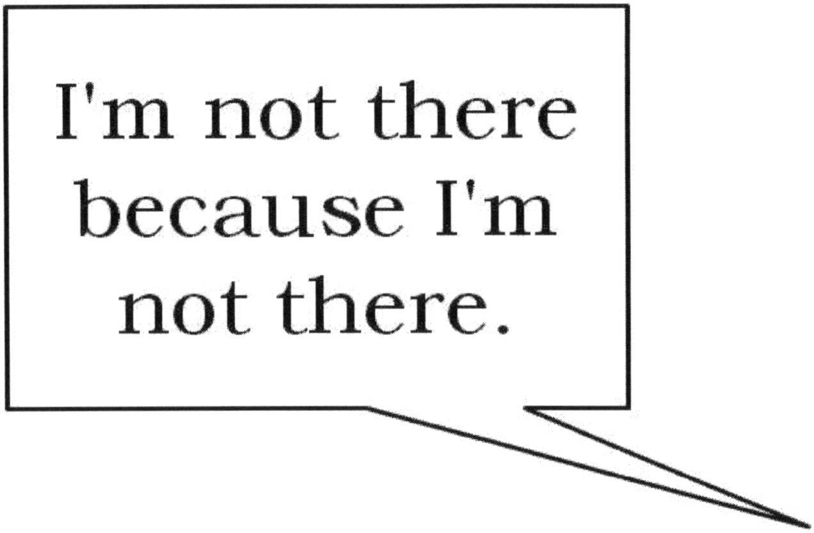
I'm not there because I'm not there.

But for what purpose did you believe that you needed to have these four water filtration devices for your store?

For the water.

The guy in Montana was a guy. I mean, he was a legitimate guy.

PART 13: WHAT?

Is there anything that you contemplated doing previously that you haven't to date done that you intend to do?

Well, the hole had been replaced by that point in time.

The bike had no intentions of being seen or ridden.

We coming right back to the same thing that has not been cleared up. Why you going to put me right back in the same boat and pour hot water on me again?

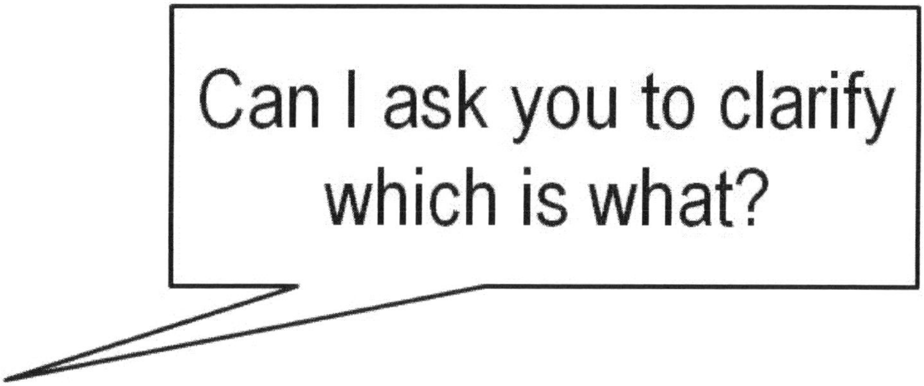
Can I ask you to clarify which is what?

Those kinds of things, I drew on Tim.

So far as you can recall, have things just kind of bumped along very smoothly in Texas from 1994 to the present?

PART 14: ATTORNEYS, CLIENTS AND LAWSUITS

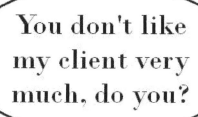

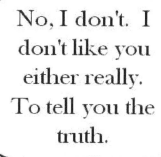

What did you do
to prepare for this
deposition today?

I got up and put
my clothes on.

We're going to stop this deposition at some point. I'm not doing it now. But we're not going to give a deposition for the rest of our lives.

I never said we didn't like them.

Do you sue people 12 times that you like?

So are you saying that if someone else does something illegal, you can do something illegal, too?
No. You can't if you don't get caught—you can if you don't get caught.
You can if you don't get caught?
Yeah. That's what their trouble is, they're getting caught.

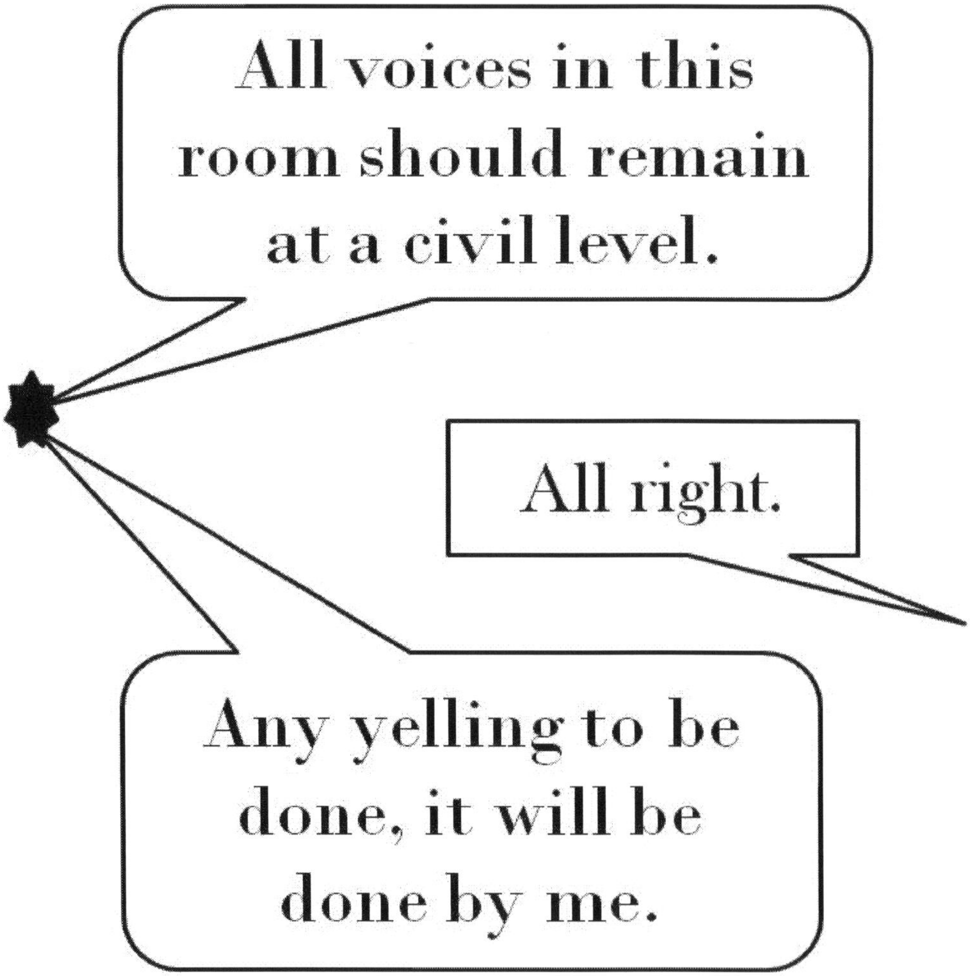
All voices in this room should remain at a civil level.
All right.
Any yelling to be done, it will be done by me.

And so me not really—
not legal minded, don't
know, you know, what
I can and can't say. I
don't—I typically don't
say anything because
that usually keeps me
out of trouble.

I was saying maybe I'm not a good expert for you because I'm an honest expert.

I don't know if I'm really supposed to say what I'm thinking.

Oh, yeah, you are. Just let it hang out. It's a lawsuit. It's okay.

This is a formal proceeding, but it doesn't have to be a jerk proceeding; okay?

PART 15:
CORRESPONDENCE

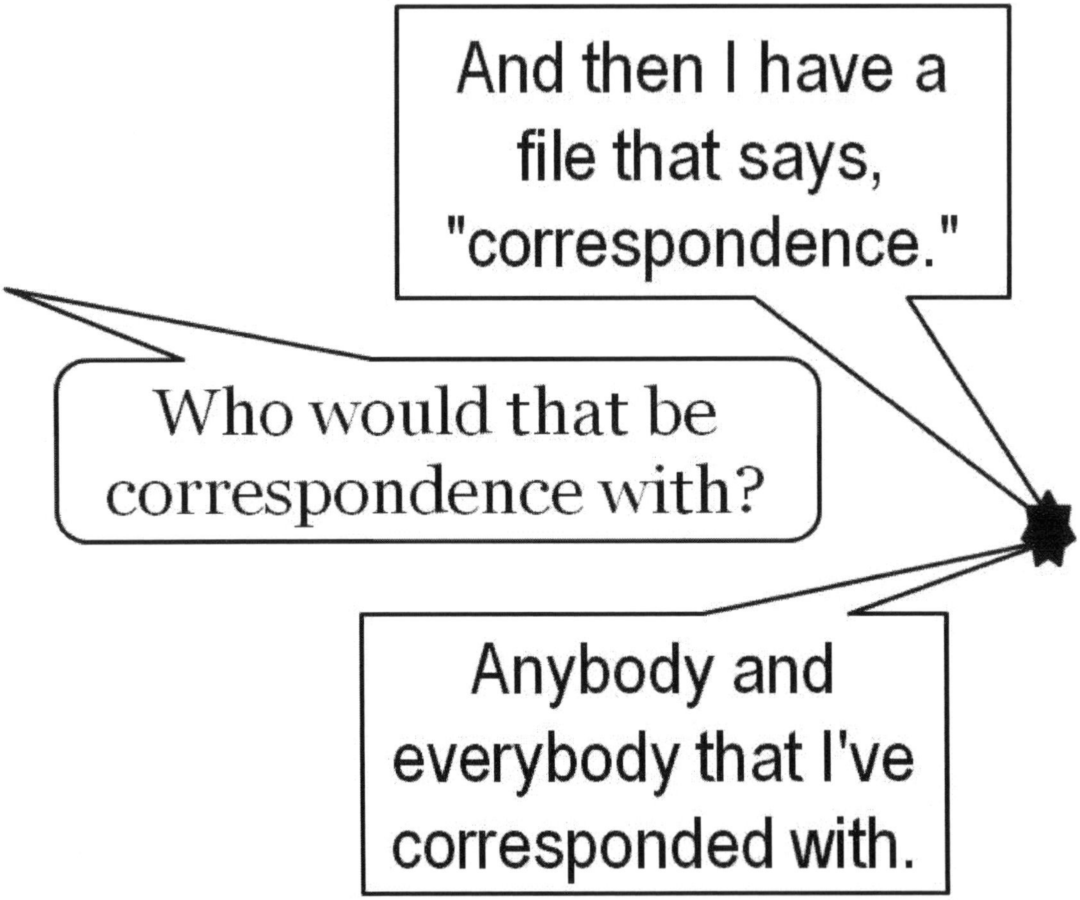
And then I have a file that says, "correspondence."
Who would that be correspondence with?
Anybody and everybody that I've corresponded with.

I see e-mail correspondence between you and Jim. And it says, "Thanks for your help." What was this about?

I believe he was thanking me for my help.

But I think everyone in the world, generally, who gets mail and wants to know what it says should open it up and should look at it.

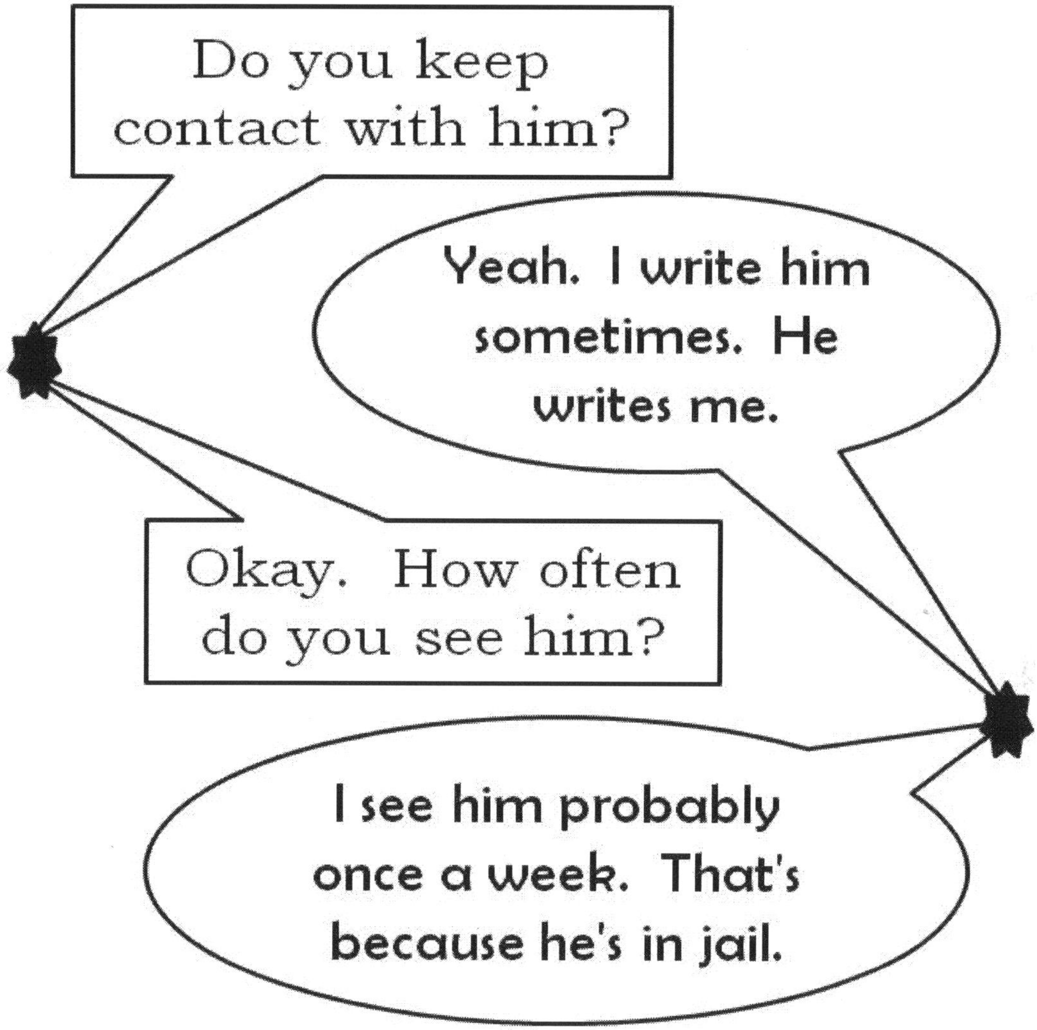
Do you keep contact with him?
Yeah. I write him sometimes. He writes me.
Okay. How often do you see him?
I see him probably once a week. That's because he's in jail.

PART 16:
TO YOUR HEALTH

Workmen's comp sent me to Tulsa to some doctor. I ain't sure what his name was. I can't remember it.

A doctor for the insurance company?

No. For the silicosis.

I mean, I wasn't a believer in ADHD until Joey came along.

I was dizzy and blurry.

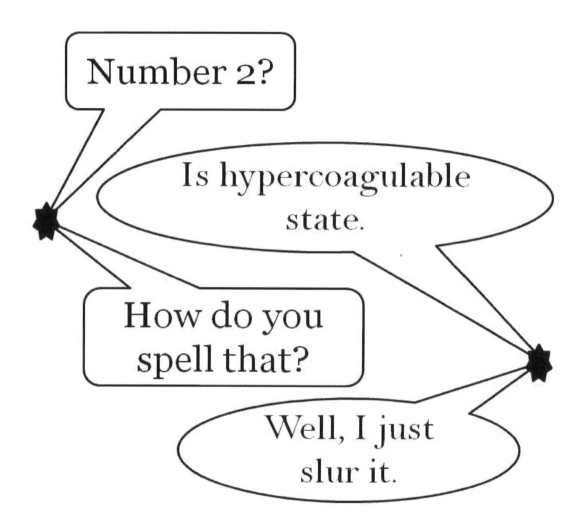

PART 17: LET'S NOT MINCE WORDS

Don't speculate if you're just going to be speculating.

You don't have to say, "Yes, sir," to me. I say, "Yes, sir," to you, okay?

Yes, sir.

Is that yes?

That is yes. Yes, it is. That is yes.

So if they're incorrect, then you relied on incorrect information; is that correct?

All is an all-encompassing word.

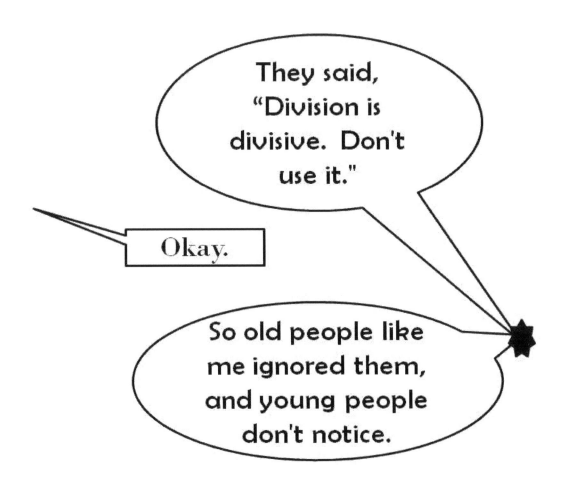

PART 18: AIRHEADS

Tell me what I'm supposed to assume again.

Do you have any understanding?

No.

She may not be as smart as the next person, but that doesn't mean anything.

I wasn't planning on thinking about anything.

I'm sure you think I understood that.
Okay.
But the problem is I didn't.

Have you ever been convicted of a crime?
No, sir. Not to my knowledge.

No, I was not aware of much at all in 1985.

Do you think that's caused you any embarrassment or loss of reputation?

If it has, I'm not aware of it.

I attempted to pay attention.

But like I say, I can't enter his personal life because I am not personally him.

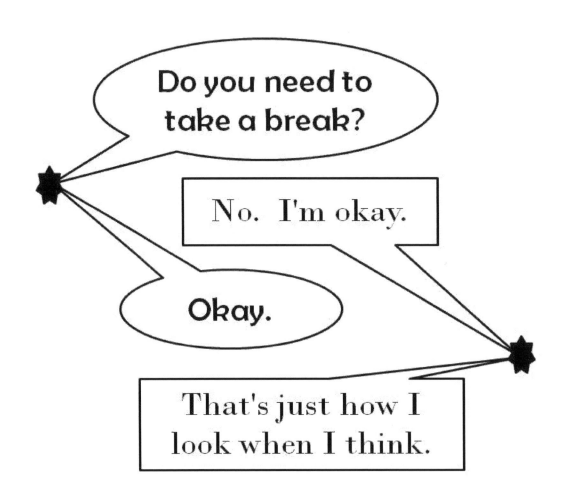

I'll try not to confuse me.

PART 19:
LIFE AND DEATH

Did you ever tell the judge about it?

No. He's dead.

Do you have a certain time frame that you have to have that done by?

Sometime before I die.

If I use old terminology, excuse me. I'm getting old, too.

Who did you go to lunch with today?

Went with them and my daughter and my mother. I mean my wife. Sorry about that. Don't you tell her I said that. Well, it might be good. My mother's 122.

And where does Joe live?

He's in the grave yard.

He is deceased, and he took all of his institutional knowledge with him.

Is that you in this picture?

Few hairs ago, yes.

PART 20: FRIENDS AND FAMILY

I think mother's term for me is "neither-dexterous." I can't write with either hand.

Did you and she get along well?

Yeah. Yes. We got along about as good as two old women can get along.

I don't think the word "hatred" would come out of my mouth in describing my emotions. Because I don't hate my brother. And I don't hate anyone that I can think of, except perhaps Dick Cheney.

He's almost 48 years old. He needs to be on his own.

I'm intrigued by the massage parlor that your mother ran for ten years.

So am I.

And the "friend" is your beer; right?

Yes.

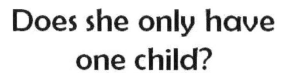

Does she only have one child?

Currently.

Is she pregnant?

She's due any minute. I hope that's not her calling telling me she's having her baby.

PART 21: HODGEPODGE

I want to
go back to
Christmas
morning.

I think with any washing machine, you would—there's an assumption that your clothes are going to get clean.

Beyond the normal common trade show association dinner, I've never had dinner.

Did she offer some constructive criticism to you?

Always. Always.

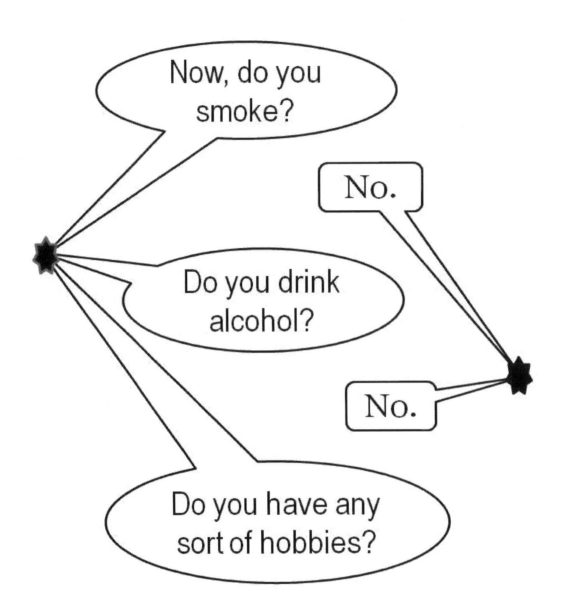

That was harder to say than I thought it was going to be.

I noticed that.

I'm going to jump around for a few minutes, and I apologize.

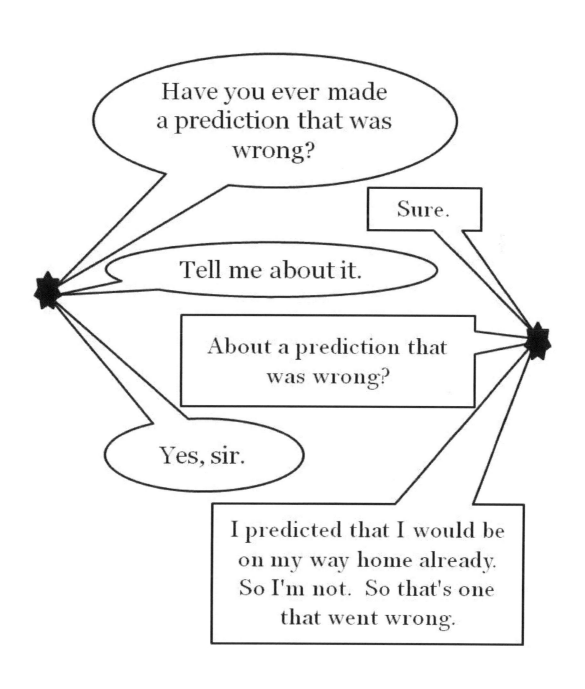

Because TDY means that you're deployed yonder; is that right?

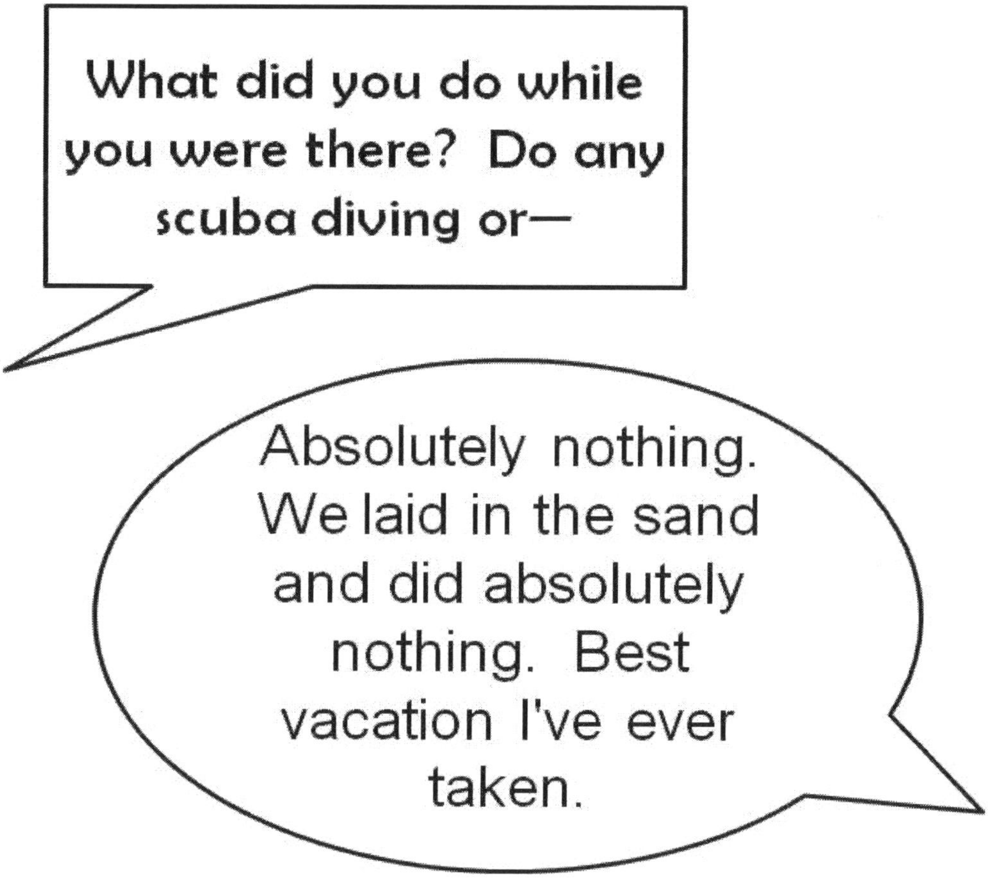
What did you do while you were there? Do any scuba diving or—
Absolutely nothing. We laid in the sand and did absolutely nothing. Best vacation I've ever taken.

We are still discovering things that aren't there.

What about weather?

The weather was actually very good during that time frame. That was another one of our drought periods.

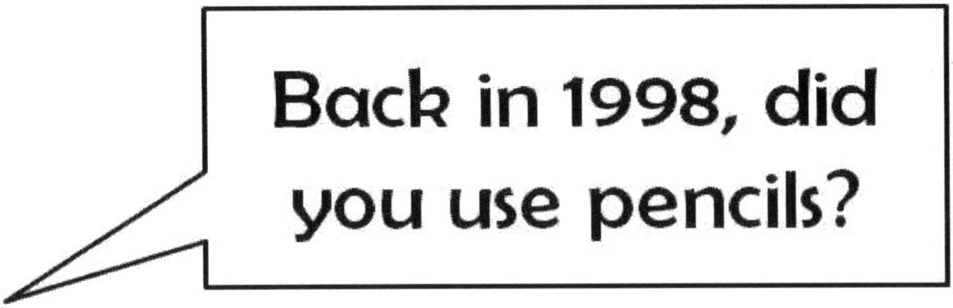
Back in 1998, did you use pencils?

Do you think you've had any emotional distress as a result of this?

I don't get emotional too much. I get mad. I don't get emotional.

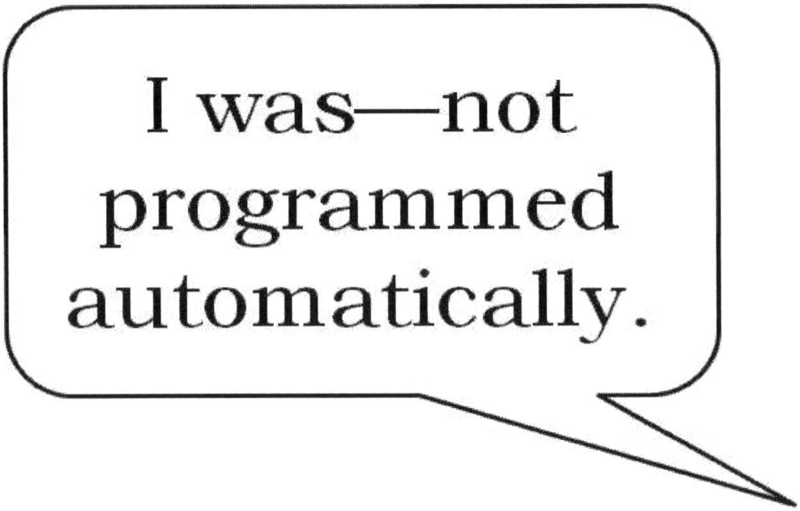
I was—not programmed automatically.

If anyone sins, we have a Counselor with the Father,
Jesus Christ, the righteous.
1 John 1:2b
World English Bible